What's Living in Your Kitchen?

Andrew Solway

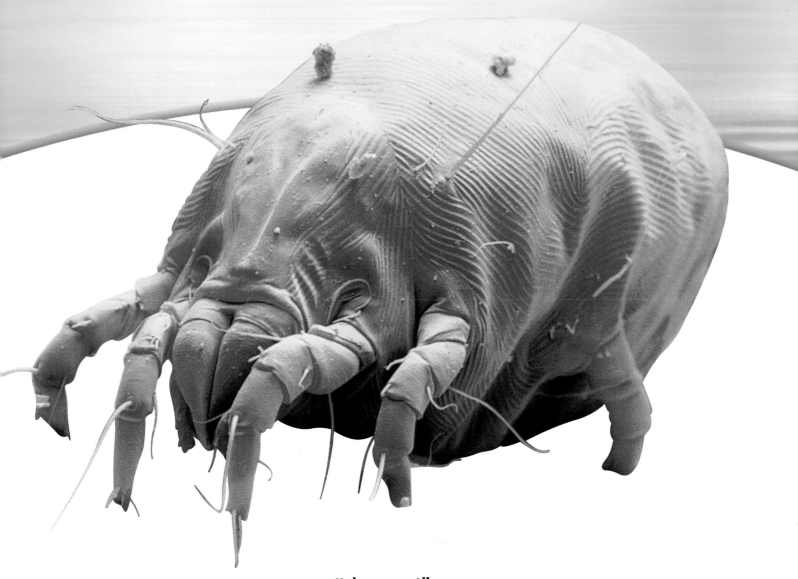

Heinemann Library
Chicago, Illinois

© 2004 Heinemann Library
a division of Reed Elsevier, Inc.
Chicago, Illinois

Customer Service 888-454-2279
Visit our website at www.heinemannlibrary.com

Designed by David Poole and Paul Myerscough
Illustrations by Geoff Ward
Originated by Dot Gradations
Printed and bound in China by South China Printing Company

09 08 07 06 05 04
10 9 8 7 6 5 4 3 2 1

Library of Congress Cataloging-in-Publication Data

Solway, Andrew.
   What's living in your kitchen? / Andrew Solway.
      v. cm. -- (Hidden life)
   Contents: Take a closer look -- Dust-eaters -- Mite pests --
Yeasts in the bread -- Microbes in the food -- Moldy food --
Food spoilage -- Stopping spoilage -- Food poisoning bacteria
-- Surface microbes -- Microbes in the drains.
   ISBN 1-4034-4844-2 (hc : lib. bdg.) -- ISBN 1-4034-5483-3
(pb)
   1. Food--Microbiology--Juvenile literature. 2. Kitchens--Sani-
tation--Juvenile literature.   [1. Microbiology. 2. Food.]
I. Title. II. Series.
QR115.S595 2004
664'.001'579--dc22

                              2003018005

Acknowledgments
The author and publishers are grateful to the following for permission to reproduce
copyright material: pp. **4t**, **19** Corbis (RF), p. **13t** (Jacqui Hurst), p. **22r** (Sally A Morgan);
pp. **4b**, **10t**, **10b**, **15** Science Photo Library (David Scharf), p. **5** (R. Maisonneuve, Publiphoto
Diffusion), p. **6b** (Medical Stock Photo), pp. **7**, **27**, **23**, **25** (Eye of Science), p. **9** (Susumu
Nishinaga), pp. **10**, **13b** (Rosenfeld Images Ltd), p. **12** (Scimat), p. **14** (Noble Proctor), p. **16**
(Prof. N. Russell), p. **17** (Martin Chillmaid), p. **20** (CAMR, Barry Dowsett), p. **21** (DrGary
Gaugler), p. **22L**, **24T** (Volker Steger), p. **24b** (Eric Grave), pp. **26**, **27b** (Sinclair Stammers);
p. **6t** Alamy Images; p. **8** Holt Studio International; p. **18** Tudor Photography.

Cover photograph of a meal mite, reproduced with permission of Science Photo Library/
Science Pictures.

Our thanks to Dr. Philip Parrillo, entomologist at the Field Museum in Chicago, for his
comments in the preparation of this book.

Every effort has been made to contact copyright holders of any material reproduced in this
book. Any omissions will be rectified in subsequent printings if notice is given to the
publishers.

Some words are shown in bold, **like this.** You can find out
what they mean by looking in the glossary.

Contents

Take a Closer Look 4

Dust Eaters .6

Mite Pests .8

Yeasts in the Bread 10

Microbes in Other Foods 12

Moldy Food 14

Food Spoilage 16

Stopping Spoilage 18

Food-Poisoning Bacteria 20

Surface Microbes 22

Microbes in the Drains 24

Wheel Animals 26

Table of Sizes 28

Glossary 30

More Books to Read 31

Index 32

Many of the photos in this book were taken using a microscope.
In the captions you may see a number that tells you how much
they have been enlarged. For example, a photo marked
"(x200)" is about 200 times bigger than in real life.

Take a Closer Look

Modern kitchens are bright, clean places. We regularly wipe down surfaces, we keep foods that might spoil in the refrigerator, and we cook food to make it safe to eat. It seems that there is nowhere for living creatures to survive. But look closely, and you will find plenty of hidden life.

This kitchen may look empty, but up close there is hidden life everywhere.

This magnified view (x2260) of a kitchen scrubbing pad shows thousands of bacteria (tiny ovals) on the pad fibers.

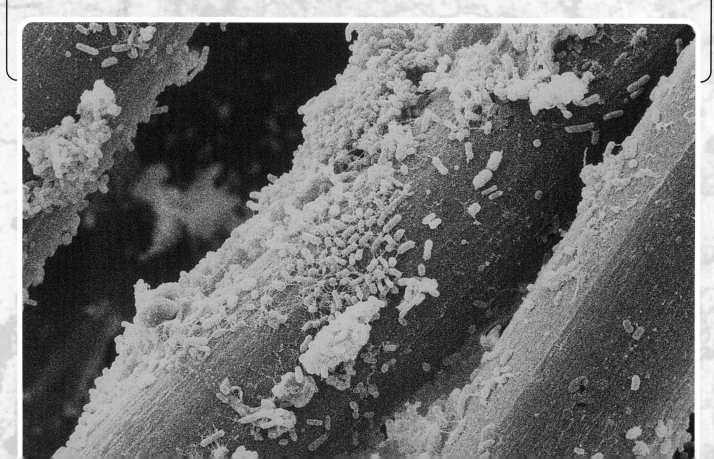

All life, no matter how tiny, needs water and food to survive. Kitchens have plenty of both these things. It's surprising just how many living things manage to find food in even the cleanest and shiniest of kitchens.

Getting up close

Larger insects are occasional visitors to any kitchen. But in most kitchens there are some much smaller insects and minibeasts that we never notice. Most of them live off the crumbs of food that get overlooked, but some can survive on dust!

Closer still

If you looked around your kitchen with a microscope, you would start to find all kinds of **microbes.** Most of these creatures are made of just a single living **cell.** The smallest and most widespread of these one-celled microbes are

bacteria. But there are also other kinds, such as **fungi**—relatives of the mushrooms you may have had on a pizza.

Eating microbes

We tend to think of microbes as harmful germs, but some microbes are essential for making our food and drink. We use fungi to make bread, beer, and wine, and bacteria to make cheese and yogurt.

MICROSCOPES

The reason we know about the many kinds of hidden life is because scientists have used microscopes to study them. A light microscope—the kind of microscope that you might have used at school or at home—can magnify things up to 1,800 times. But to get a close look at really tiny things such as bacteria, you need an **electron microscope.** This can magnify objects up to 500,000 times.

Electron microscopes are expensive and complicated machines that are used mostly by scientists.

If you look closely, you will find that dust is made up of all kinds of things. There are bits of fluff from clothing. There are hairs and pieces of dead insects. There are crumbs of food, ashes from burning, wood shavings, **pollen,** and perhaps soil. But one of the main things in household dust is bits of your skin.

Skin-eating mites

Our skin is always replacing itself, and as new skin is formed the old skin flakes off. These skin flakes are the favorite food of creatures called dust mites.

Mites are relatives of spiders. This means they have eight legs instead of six. Dust mites live in carpets, furnishings, cracks, and dusty corners. They mainly eat human skin, but they also dine on almost any other food that they find.

On average, dust mites live about a month. They take about a month to grow from eggs to adults, going through four different

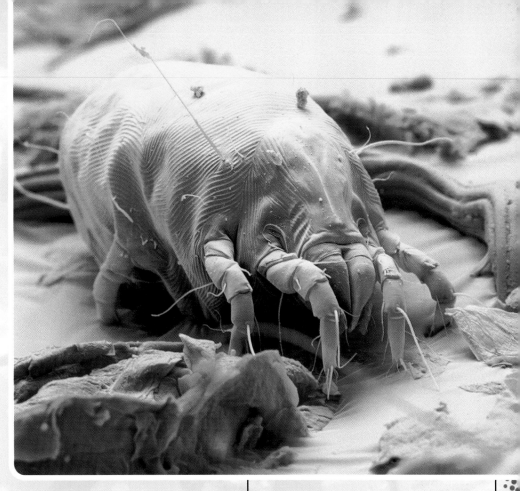

stages in the process. A female dust mite lays 40 to 100 eggs in her lifetime.

Dust mite problems

Dust mites themselves are completely harmless to humans. But dust mite droppings and the skins they shed when they **molt** become part of the dust in the house, and for some

This dust mite is feeding on flakes of skin (x637). Dust mites have no eyes. They find their way around by touch and smell.

people this can be a problem. Chemicals in them can cause **allergies** in sensitive people. The allergy may be nothing worse than a few sneezes, but some people may get **asthma.**

NO NEED TO DRINK

Dust mites never need to drink. The air around us contains a certain amount of **water vapor,** and dust mites can absorb some of this water vapor as they breathe. But if the air gets too dry, the mites cannot get enough water vapor and soon die.

Mite Pests

Dust mites are not the only mites you might find in the kitchen. Other kinds of mites are pests, too, because they prefer the food we eat to dust and skin.

Some mites are pests of food crops, and several kinds are also pests of household food. Flour mites and cheese mites are two of these "mitey" pests.

As with dust mites, flour mites go through four different stages before becoming adults. If food is scarce or if the air is dry, young flour mites may go into a **dormant** resting state. When they are resting, the outside of their bodies harden, and the mites hardly move. Mites in this resting stage can survive **pesticides** that would kill a normal mite, and they can live without food or water for up to several months.

Flour mites

Flour mites feed on all kinds of food but prefer flour. Flour is most likely to get infested with mites if large amounts are kept in warm, slightly damp conditions. A single female mite can lay up to 800 eggs, and it takes only about 10 days for the eggs to become adults, so one mite can quickly become a serious **infestation.** Flour infested with mites has a sharp smell and causes an upset stomach if eaten.

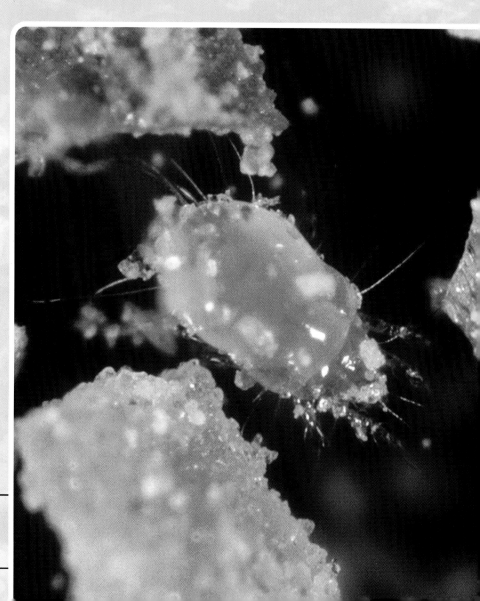

This flour mite is feeding on pieces of bran flour.

Cheese mites

Cheese mites are also sometimes found in flour, but they prefer cheese. As with flour mites, cheese mites prefer warm, damp conditions, so cheese kept in the refrigerator is unlikely to become infested. If cheese does get infested with mites, it becomes covered in a gray powder, which is a mixture of mites, mite droppings, and their shed skins.

Most cheeses are spoiled if they become infested with mites. However, in the Altenberg region of Germany the makers of one type of cheese deliberately add cheese mites to the newly made cheese and then leave it to ripen. When the cheese is covered with a gray powdery coating, it is ready to eat. Not surprisingly, this kind of cheese is not everyone's favorite!

TINY HITCHHIKERS

To move out of a place where conditions are not good, mites often hitch a ride on a larger creature. Many kinds of mites move from place to place by clinging onto the legs or other parts of a large insect.

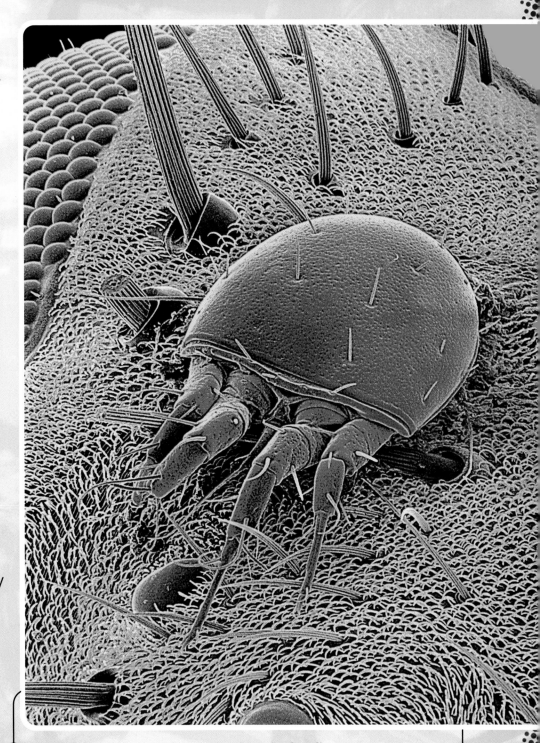

A mite hitches a ride on the head of a fly. (You can see the fly's eye at the top left.) Usually this hitchhiking does not affect the insect carrier, but large numbers of mites can weigh it down or even kill it.

Yeasts in the Bread

If you have ever made bread, you will know that you use **yeast** to make the bread rise. Yeast is a tiny living thing—a type of **fungus.** Most people use dried yeast to make bread. Yeast can survive being dried out because it goes into a resting state, similar to the way flour mites do. If you add warm water and sugar, the yeast becomes active again.

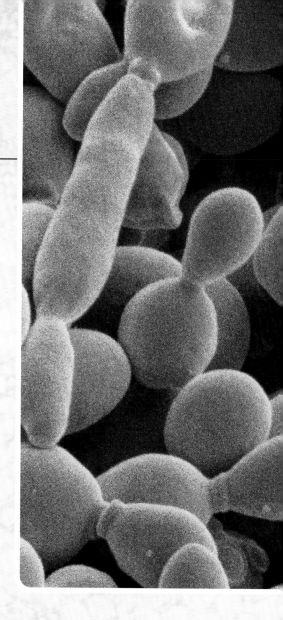

Bread rises because of the carbon dioxide produced by tiny yeast cells in the bread dough.

Yeasts in bread
Yeast is a very tiny creature made of just a single **cell.** If you keep yeast cells warm and give them sugary food, they will grow and reproduce. They break down the sugar to get energy. A waste product of this process is **carbon dioxide** gas.

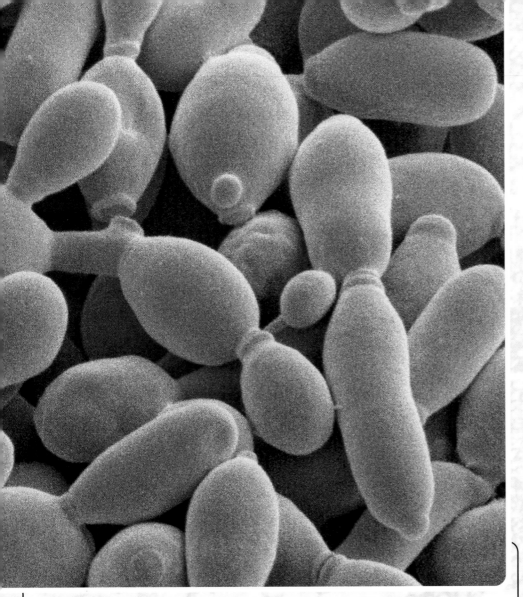

Yeasts in beer

When yeast cells break down sugars, they produce alcohol in addition to carbon dioxide. So yeast is also used to make beers and wines. The yeast is **fermented** (see box) with a sugary liquid to produce alcohol. In beer-making, the sugary liquid is usually made from barley, while in wine-making the liquid is grape juice.

The type of yeast used for bread-making produces a lot of carbon dioxide but not much alcohol, while beer-making yeast does the opposite.

❶ Above is a magnified view (x8277) of the kind of yeast used in beer-making and baking. Yeast cells reproduce by budding off new cells. Some budding cells can be seen in this photo.

Bread dough is basically flour and water mixed to make a thick dough. Yeast added to this mixture uses the **starch** in the flour as food and begins to produce carbon dioxide. Bubbles of gas get trapped in the dough, making it light and airy. When you put the bread in the oven, the yeast cells continue to grow and produce carbon dioxide for a short time. But before long the bread becomes too hot, and the yeast is killed.

LIFE WITHOUT AIR

Most living things need **oxygen** to help them get energy from their food. This is why they have to breathe. But yeasts and some other **microbes** can get energy from their food without using oxygen. This process is known as fermentation. Alcohol and carbon dioxide are the waste products.

Microbes in Other Foods

Have you ever opened a bottle of milk, sniffed it and realized that the milk is spoiled? Milk spoils because **bacteria** grow in it and make it sour. But we get those bacteria to work for us when making cheese and yogurt.

Cheese and yogurt are both made by **fermenting** milk. The process is similar to that used for bread making, except that bacteria are used rather than **yeast.** Bacteria are added to milk, and they use sugars in the milk as food. Waste products that the bacteria produce as they grow change the milk in useful ways.

Lactobacillus bulgaricus *(the orange rods at the top left)* and Streptococcus thermophilis *(the chains of orange balls)* can be used to make yogurt and cheese.

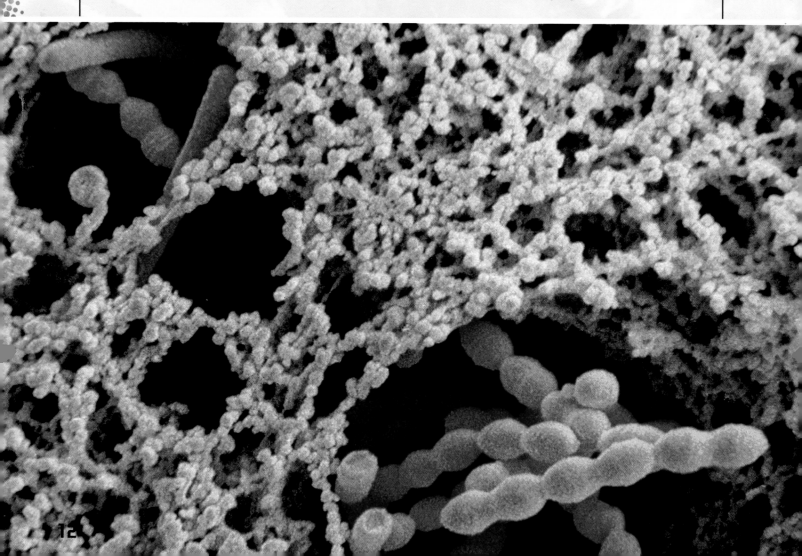

In some cheeses, a **mold fungus** is added as well as the bacteria. In blue cheese the mold gives the cheese its blue streaks.

Yogurt making

To make yogurt, milk is left to ferment with a certain type of bacteria. The waste product that the bacteria produces is an **acid** (lactic acid). The acid is what gives yogurt its sharp taste. This is similar to what happens when milk spoils, but in sour milk there are also many other kinds of bacteria, and some of them produce unpleasant tastes.

Cheese making

In cheese making the same kind of bacteria as in yogurt making is used. As with yogurt, the bacteria produce acid, which **curdles** the milk and gives it a sharp taste. But a substance called **rennet** is also added to the milk, which makes it separate into a white solid (curds) and a thin, watery liquid (whey).

In the next stage, the whey is drained off, and the curds are cut up and salted. The salt slows the fermentation reaction, so that the cheese does not become too sharp-tasting.

The curds are squeezed in a press to remove more liquid. Then the cheese is left to ripen for a few weeks or months. During ripening, the bacteria in the cheese continue to grow slowly and help give the cheese its flavor.

Cheeses ripens in a cool storage room. Ripe cheese still has living bacteria in it, but they are killed by the acid in our stomach when we eat the cheese.

Moldy Food

We say that when food spoils it is moldy. This is because it is often **molds** that spoil food. Molds are **fungi,** related to mushrooms and to the **yeasts** used for making bread and beer.

*The green mold on this orange is caused by a mold called Penicillium. One type of Penicillium is important medically, because the **antibiotic** penicillin is made from it. Penicillium uses the antibiotic as a chemical weapon to get rid of **bacteria** that compete with it for food.*

Going moldy

So what happens when, for instance, an orange goes moldy? The mold begins as a small white spot, which then spreads. Once the spot gets to a certain size, it begins to turn green at the center, and the green area quickly grows. After four or five days, the whole orange may be covered in green mold.

Like other fungi, molds are made up of tiny threads, or **hyphae,** and they reproduce by releasing **spores** (see box). The white spot at the start of the infection is formed by a tangle of growing hyphae. The white mold then turns green as spores begin to form on tiny stalks above the body of the fungus.

Doing an important job

Molds are a nuisance because they can spoil our food, but they also do an important job. They are

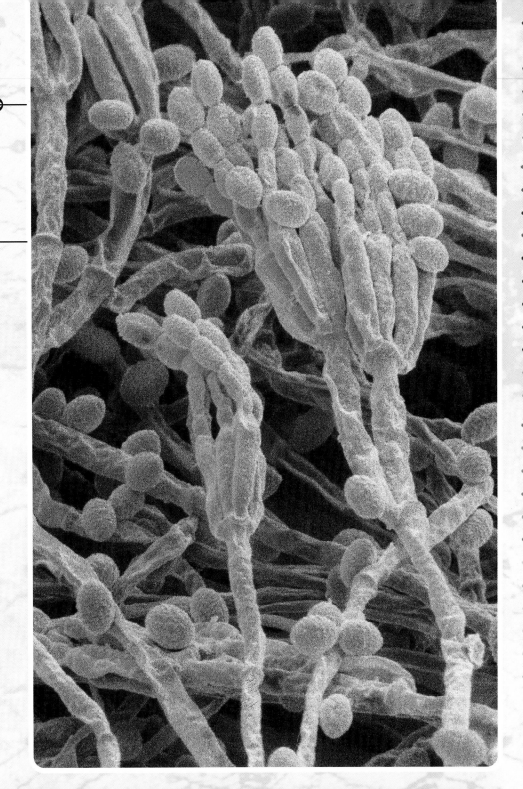

This magnified photo (x2855) shows the spore-producing structures of penicillium. The round shapes on the ends of the hyphae are spores.

part of nature's recycling system, which breaks down the bodies of dead animals and plants and releases their **nutrients** back into the environment.

Obviously, we do not want molds to recycle the fruit and bread that we wish to eat. But molds also break down tough materials such as wood, and unpleasant ones such as animal droppings. Only molds and other fungi can digest some of the chemicals in wood and turn them into useful nutrients.

FUNGUS FACTS

Fungi are neither plants nor animals. They do not make their own food as plants do and they do not eat food the way animals do. Instead they grow into their food and absorb nutrients from it. Most fungi either grow on dead or rotting material, or they are **parasites**.

Fungi usually grow as microscopic threads called hyphae. The body of the fungus is a tangle of these threads. They reproduce by making millions of tiny spores.

Food Spoilage

When foods spoil, **molds** are not the only ones to blame. They get a lot of help from **bacteria.** There are always small numbers of bacteria on food, but once they begin to grow and reproduce, they make food taste bad.

There are bacteria around us all the time. They live on your skin, on your pets, and on other animals and plants. Bacteria float in the air and grow on most of the surfaces that are found in the house.

Bacteria are found on fresh food, and if conditions are right (see below), they will spread. A population of about a million bacteria is enough to make food taste spoiled.

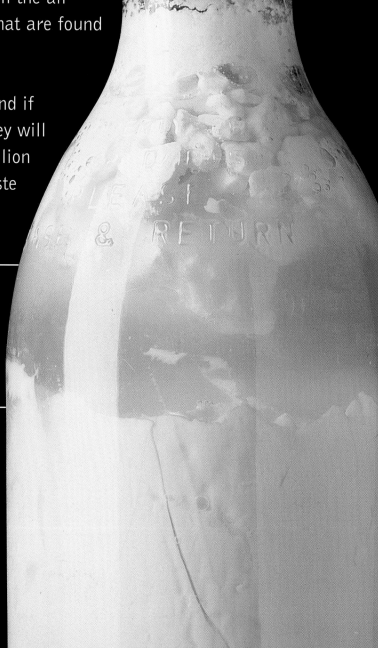

*Before it is sold, milk is usually **pasteurized** (heated gently) to get rid of bacteria. Even so, milk spoils very quickly if it is left out of the refrigerator.*

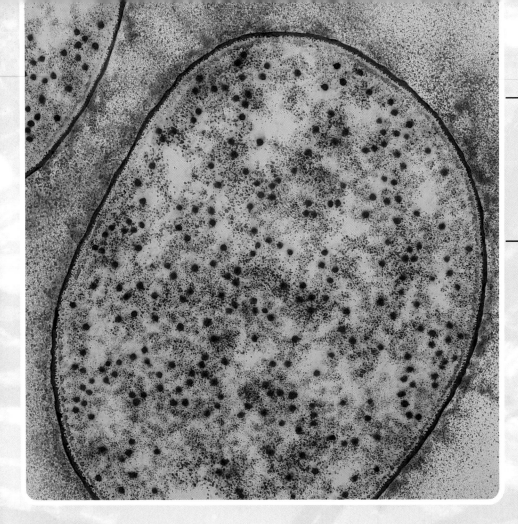

Psychrobacter *bacteria* (x108,000) *like this one grow well in cold conditions. They can spoil food even in the refrigerator.*

This is fine in yogurt and cheese, but it makes many foods taste sour and unpleasant.

What conditions cause spoilage?

Many different kinds of bacteria cause spoilage. Which kinds develop on food depends on how the food is kept. For instance, many bacteria grow best at normal temperatures, from about 40 °F to 70 °F (5 °C to 20 °C), and will do well if food is left out in normal conditions. However, some bacteria grow well at temperatures as low as 32 °F (0 °C), and they can cause food to spoil even in the refrigerator. Other kinds grow best in hot conditions, and they can spoil food that has been cooked and left in a warm place.

How do bacteria spoil food?

A bacterium does not have a mouth to eat its food with. Instead, it releases chemicals called **enzymes** into the food. The enzymes break the food down into **nutrients** that the bacterium can absorb. One of the things that happens when food spoils is that it gets mushy or watery. This is caused by bacterial enzymes.

Like people and other animals, bacteria produce wastes. These are often another cause of food spoilage. Some bacteria produce **acid** as waste.

BREEDING BACTERIA

Large numbers of bacteria can build up on food incredibly quickly. Under ideal conditions, some kinds of bacteria can reproduce every twenty minutes. At this speed, a single bacterium could produce several million others within eight hours.

Stopping Spoilage

People have developed many different ways of making food keep longer without spoiling. Most of these methods are based on understanding how **microbes** spread and grow.

Cooling and drying

Like other living things, most **bacteria** grow best in warm conditions, though as we saw on page 17, some bacteria like the cold. Bacteria also need water in order to grow and multiply.

One way we can stop foods from spoiling is to keep them in the refrigerator or freezer. The low temperatures kill many kinds of bacteria, and even those that survive cannot grow quickly.

Since bacteria need water, another way to stop food from spoiling is to keep it dry. Fresh food naturally contains a lot of water, so to really make this work you have to dry the food. For thousands of years people have been preserving food by drying it. More recently we have developed new dried foods such as powdered soup and dry milk.

Food can be made to last longer by various ways. Pickling, drying, canning, and freezing are a few of them.

Pickling and salting

Most kinds of bacteria do not like **acid** conditions—this is one of the reasons that cheese keeps longer than milk. Pickling foods in vinegar makes them very acidic, so they keep longer. You can pickle all kinds of foods, from eggs to fish to apricots.

Another way of stopping bacteria from growing is to add salt to food. The most obvious salted foods are nuts and chips. Butter is often salted, and so are some kinds of meat and fish.

Canning and irradiation

When food is canned, it is heated to get rid of the bacteria and then put in sealed cans so that no new bacteria can get in. Many kinds of canned foods keep for years without spoiling.

A more recent way of getting rid of bacteria on food is irradiation. This

A cannery plant is a very clean and sterile place where no bacteria can grow.

involves shooting food with gamma rays (a type of radiation similar to X rays). Irradiation kills almost all bacteria on food, so it will keep much longer. But many people do not like the idea of eating irradiated food, and some people think it is harmful.

Food-Poisoning Bacteria

A family has soup for dinner, and someone forgets to put the leftovers in the refrigerator. The next day, Dad heats up the remains of the soup for lunch. Later he feels awful: he is sick and has a high temperature. The soup was full of food-poisoning **bacteria.**

Cooking kills most bacteria, but if you leave soup out overnight a few bacteria might get into it. In warm, wet soup, bacteria can multiply very quickly. Even large numbers of some kinds of bacteria will do no harm, but other kinds can make you ill.

Bacterial poisons

Different bacteria cause food poisoning in different ways. Some kinds produce toxins (poisons) as they grow in the food, and these make you ill.

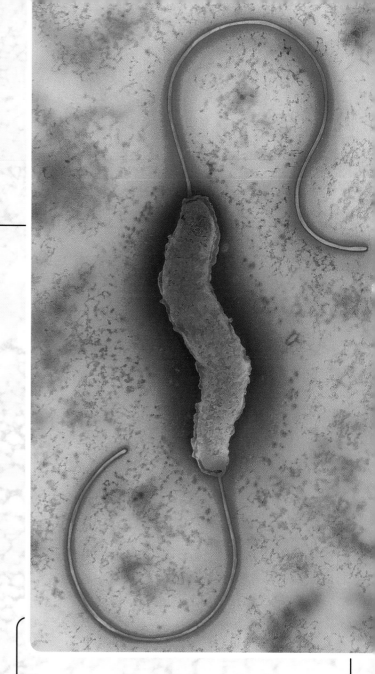

Campylobacter (x33,530) is another common cause of food poisoning. It is an unusual bacterium because of its spiral shape. It has long, whiplike tails at either end that enable it to move quickly.

Staphylococcus aureus can cause food poisoning in this way. This bacterium is most often found in cooked meat or chicken. Large numbers of the bacteria need to grow before infected food will make you ill, but if this happens, heating will not get rid of the toxin.

Tough survivors

Other bacteria only need to be present in small numbers on the food because they survive in your gut and multiply there. They cause damage to your gut lining, and this is what makes you ill. Symptoms of this kind of food poisoning show up a few days after you eat because it takes that long for the bacteria to multiply in the gut.

The bacteria *Salmonella* and *Escherichia coli* cause food poisoning in this way. *Salmonella* is found in many kinds of food, but especially in raw meat and eggs. *E. coli* exist in several different types, or strains. Some of these normally live in the lower part of our gut without causing ill effects. However, other types that are found in raw meat, **unpasteurized** milk, and **contaminated** water can cause serious food poisoning.

Avoiding food poisoning

If you are careful about how you prepare your food, you are unlikely to get food poisoning. Wash raw food well before you eat it, and check that meat and chicken are properly cooked before you eat them. And make sure you do not leave soup or any other cooked food out overnight.

Clostridium botulinum *is a very rare cause of food poisoning, but it can be deadly. It produces an extremely powerful toxin, one of the most poisonous substances known.*

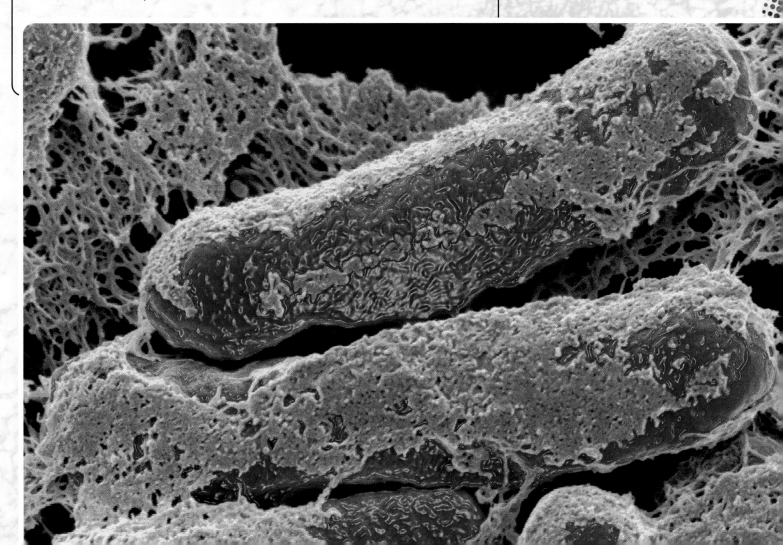

Surface Microbes

No matter how clean a kitchen looks, there will be **microbes** everywhere. In most places there are only a few, and without food and water they will not multiply. But in some parts of the kitchen, **bacteria** grow in large numbers. One place is in the garbage—another is on chopping boards.

Bacteria are always landing on kitchen surfaces or being transferred there from your skin. Most of these bacteria do not multiply because there is no food for them. Many microbes dry out and die on these surfaces (although they are soon replaced). However, some bacteria go into a resting state until conditions improve (see box).

The surface of a chopping board has plenty of grooves and cracks where bacteria and food particles can get stuck.

Many people separate out their kitchen scraps to go into the garden compost. A scrap bucket needs a good lid, because it is an ideal breeding ground for bacteria.

Microbe hangouts

Microbes grow in large numbers in some parts of the kitchen. One place bacteria often appear is in the garbage. Here there is plenty of food for them, and it is often damp. Other places are on kitchen cloths, sponges, and dish towels. These places are often damp or wet, and tiny food particles get caught in them.

Chopping boards have many grooves and holes where bacteria can build up. Cracks or chips in dishes or wooden spoons can be microbe traps. And **mold** can grow on damp paint or wallpaper.

Controlling microbes

One of the best ways to keep the numbers of microbes down in the kitchen is to wash your hands before preparing food. But make sure you dry them well, because dampness helps microbes

to spread. Also, change dish towels, sponges, and cloths regularly and wash chopping boards with hot water and detergent.

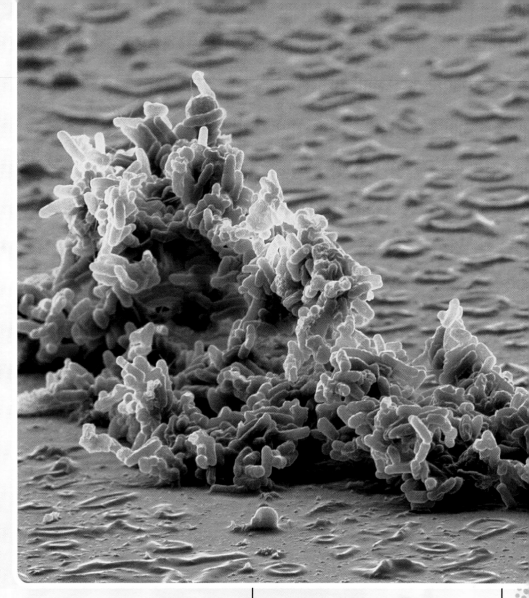

Bacteria found on kitchen surfaces come from many sources. These Enterobacter cloacae bacteria (x3770) are normally found in the gut.

BACTERIAL SPORES

Some bacteria can form thick-coated **spores** when conditions are not right for them to live and grow. Inside the spore, the bacterium lies **dormant**. It can survive drying out, low and high temperatures, and harmful chemicals. If conditions improve, a new bacterium grows from the spore. The spores of some bacteria can survive for hundreds of years.

Microbes in the Drains

Have you ever seen someone cleaning out the waste pipe of the kitchen sink? The inside of the pipe is often coated with a layer of smelly slime. This slime contains many **microbes** known as a **biofilm.**

This is a micrograph of a slightly scratched drain in a kitchen sink. Lime deposits trap dirt and encourage the growth of bacteria.

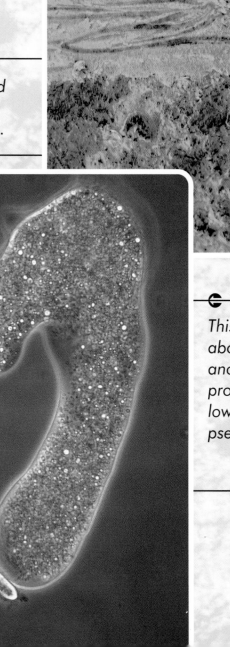

This amoeba is about to capture another, smaller protozoan (at lower right) using a pseudopod (x240).

Biofilms form quickly on wet surfaces where there is a supply of food. Kitchen drains are ideal places, because wastewater from the kitchen sink includes material that microbes can feed on. Biofilms can also form on the hulls of ships, on our teeth—even on contact lenses.

How biofilms form

Biofilms are first formed by **bacteria.** They attach to the wet surface and begin to grow. As the bacteria multiply, they begin to produce large amounts of sticky slime. They glue themselves together to form tall towers and mushroom shapes. Between the towers are water channels, which allow water and food to reach the bacteria.

In addition to cementing them together, the slime protects the bacteria from the surroundings. Such chemicals as disinfectant and bleach are much less effective against bacteria protected by this slime coating. Brushing and scrubbing is needed to get rid of them.

Microbe grazers

Once a sticky sludge begins to grow and thicken, other microbes arrive to eat the biofilm. Most of these microbes belong to a group called **protozoans.**

Amoebas are usually the first protozoans to arrive. They move over a surface by stretching out long, fingerlike structures called **pseudopods** and anchoring them to the surface, then pulling themselves forward. To feed, they flow around a bacterium or other food and then surround it completely.

Protozoans that arrive later are called **ciliates.** They have many tiny hairlike structures called **cilia,** which beat backward and forward. They use cilia to swim and to capture food.

A ciliate (green) and bacteria (red and blue) grow in a compost heap (x1785). Ciliates often use their cilia to move food, including bacteria, into their mouths.

Wheel Animals

Bacteria and one-**celled** creatures are not the only **microbes** in drain slime. There are tiny animals, too. Rotifers are a group of animals with a circle of **cilia** around their mouth.

Rotifers are not just found in drains. Over 2,000 kinds of rotifers live just about anywhere there is fresh water. Rotifers exist in such large numbers in Antarctic lakes that they turn the water red. But they can also live in a drain or a patch of damp mud.

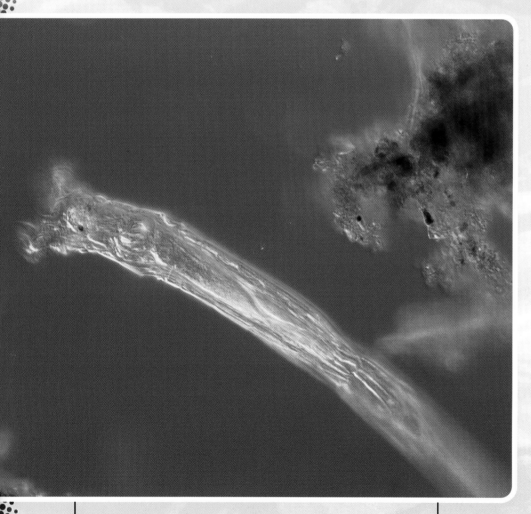

Rotifers use strong muscles to suck prey into their stomachs (x250).

Rotifers

Though they are as small as many **protozoans,** rotifers are actually multicelled animals. They have one or more light-sensing organs, muscles, and a simple gut. Many kinds have soft, see-through bodies, but some have a shell.

Rotifers get their name from the one or two rings of cilia that surround their mouth. The cilia beat in rapid waves, which makes it look as if the whole ring is rotating like a wheel. The beating cilia draw currents of water into the rotifer's mouth.

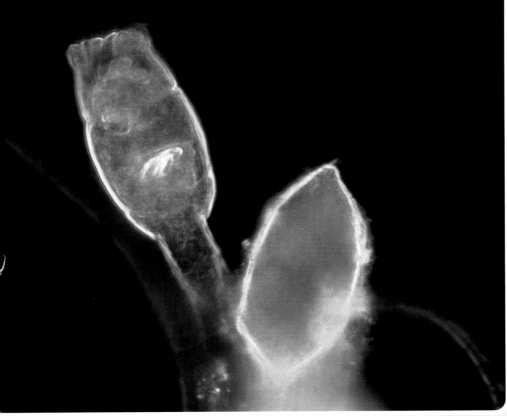

themselves. In this state they can survive a baking hot sun or freezing cold winds. They are small enough to be blown in air currents, and when they land in a wetter location they come out of their protective casing.

Rotifers can swim freely or they can attach themselves to something with their sticky foot. The kinds of rotifers in drains tend to be ones that stay attached rather than swim freely.

One of the reasons that rotifers are so successful is that they can survive long periods out of water. If the water they are in dries up, they form a protective envelope around

Conochilus rotifers form colonies by joining together in a ball. They attach to one another with their sticky foot.

Many rotifers are filter-feeders. They sift bits of food from the currents of water that they draw into their mouth. Others are **predators** that use strong muscles to suck microbes into their stomach. Food goes first to a part of the gut called the mastax, where the food is ground up.

Table of Sizes

Although all hidden life is tiny, there is a huge range of sizes. To a flea, a yeast cell seems just as tiny as the flea seems to us.

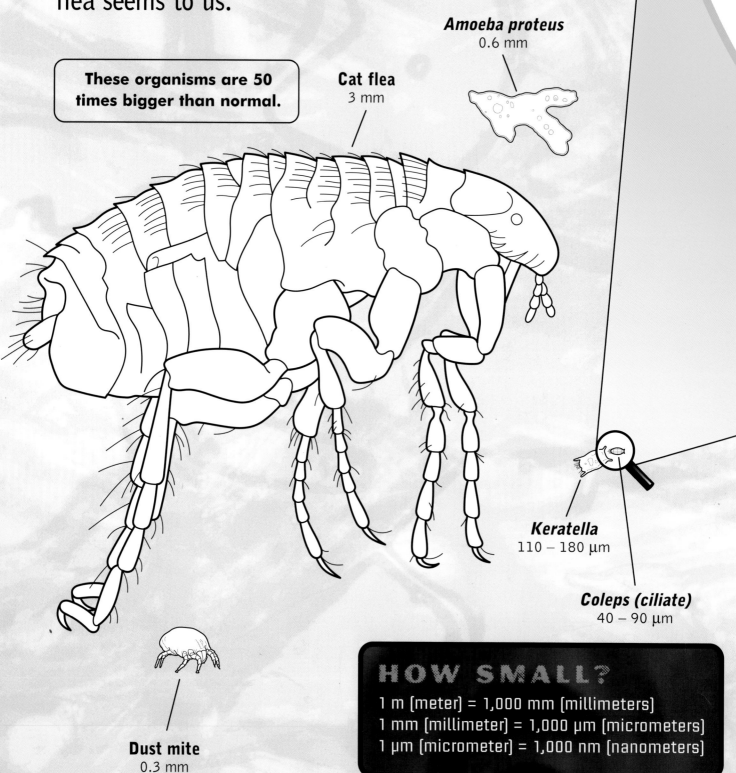

These organisms are 50 times bigger than normal.

Amoeba proteus
0.6 mm

Cat flea
3 mm

Keratella
110 – 180 μm

Coleps (ciliate)
40 – 90 μm

Dust mite
0.3 mm

HOW SMALL?

1 m (meter) = 1,000 mm (millimeters)
1 mm (millimeter) = 1,000 μm (micrometers)
1 μm (micrometer) = 1,000 nm (nanometers)

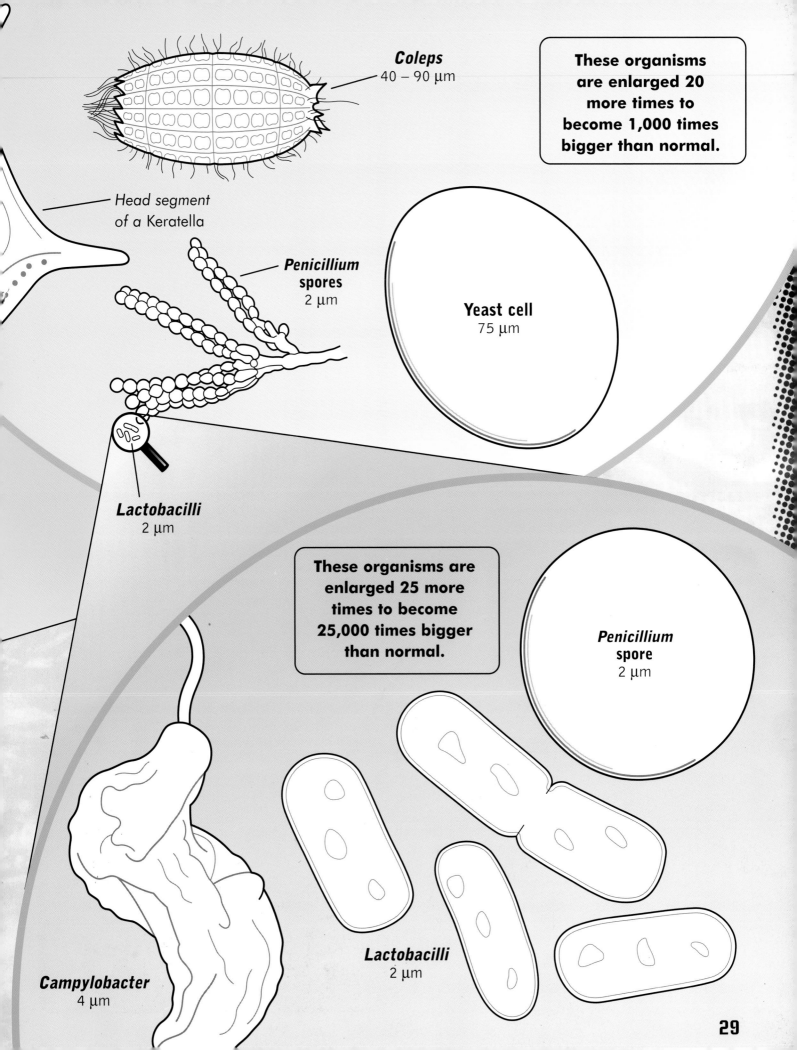

Coleps
40 – 90 µm

These organisms are enlarged 20 more times to become 1,000 times bigger than normal.

Head segment of a Keratella

Penicillium spores
2 µm

Yeast cell
75 µm

Lactobacilli
2 µm

These organisms are enlarged 25 more times to become 25,000 times bigger than normal.

Penicillium spore
2 µm

Lactobacilli
2 µm

Campylobacter
4 µm

Glossary

acid   substance that is sour, sharp, or able to dissolve other substances. Lemon juice and vinegar are acids.

allergy   condition in which the body overreacts to something that is breathed in, eaten, or gets on the skin. It can cause sneezing, rash, or sickness.

amoeba   one-celled microbe that moves and catches food by sending out fingerlike structures called pseudopods

antibiotic   drug or natural chemical that kills bacteria or stops them from growing

asthma   disease of the lungs that causes wheezing and other breathing difficulties

bacteria   microscopic living things, each one only a single cell. They are different from other one-celled creatures because they do not have a nucleus. Only one of these living things is called a bacterium.

biofilm   sticky, smelly layer of microbes and slime

carbon dioxide   gas that is found in small amounts in the air. There is also some carbon dioxide dissolved in water.

cells   building blocks of living things. Some living things are single cells, while others are made up of billions of cells working together.

cilia   tiny hairlike structures that stick out from the surface of some microbes. They can beat together in a rhythm to move the microbe along or wave food toward it. A single cilia is called a cilium.

ciliates   group of microbes that have cilia

contaminate   to become dirty or infected with disease microbes

curdle   in milk, to separate into a solid (curds) and a thin liquid (whey)

dormant   lying inactive, as if in a deep sleep

electron microscope   very powerful microscope that can magnify objects up to 500,000 times

enzymes   chemicals that are used by living cells to do such things as break down food into simple nutrients

ferment   to turn sugar in food into another substance, such as an acid or alcohol, by the action of tiny microbes

fungus   plantlike living thing such as a mushroom or a yeast. Two or more of these organisms are called fungi.

hyphae   thin, threadlike cells that make up the body of most fungi. Only one of these cells is called a hypha.

infestation   when something is overrun with harmful or irritating creatures such as insects

microbe   microscopic creature such as a bacterium, protozoan, fungus, or virus

mold   type of fungus that can grow on or in a wide range of substances, from damp plaster to cheese

molt   to shed hair, feathers, or skin

nutrient   chemical that nourishes living things

oxygen   gas that is found in the air and dissolved in water. Most living things need oxygen to live.

parasite   creature that lives on or in another living creature and takes its food from it, without giving any benefit in return and often causing harm

pasteurization   process in which milk is heated to a certain temperature for a certain period of time in order to kill harmful microbes

pesticide   chemical that is used to kill insects or other animals that are pests, for instance those that eat crops or cause disease

pollen   fine powder produced by flowers to fertilize other flowers

predator   animal that hunts and kills another animal for food.

protozoan   one-celled creature that is larger and more complicated than a bacterium

pseudopod   fingerlike projection that an amoeba sends out in order to move around and to capture food. The word means "false foot."

rennet   material made from the stomachs of young calves that is used to curdle milk in cheese making

spore   very tiny seedlike structure that a fungus uses to reproduce. A bacterial spore is a bacterium that has formed a tough outer coat to help it survive difficult conditions.

starch   the main substance in flour. Starch can be broken down by enzymes into sugars.

unpasteurized   describes a product that has not been through the pasteurization process

water vapor   water as a gas. The air around us contains some water vapor.

yeast   microscopic, one-celled fungus

More Books to Read

Kramer, Stephen. *Hidden Worlds: Looking Through a Scientist's Microscope.* Boston: Houghton Mifflin Company, 2003.

McGinty, Alice B. *Decomposers in the Food Chain.* New York: Rosen Publishing Group, 2002.

Pascoe, Elaine. *Single-Celled Organisms.* New York: Rosen Publishing, 2003.

Snedden, Robert. *Microlife: A World of Microorganisms.* Chicago: Heinemann Library, 2000.

Stewart, Gail B. *Microscopes.* Farmington Hills, Mich.: Gale Group, 2002.

Snedden, Robert. *Microlife: A World of Microorganisms.* Chicago: Heinemann Library, 2000.

Ward, Brian R. *Microscopic Life in Your Food.* North Mankato, Minn.: Smart Apple Media, 2004.

Index

acids 13, 17, 18
alcohol 11
allergies 7
amoebas 24, 25, 28
asthma 7

bacteria 4, 5, 28
  biofilms 24–5
  in drains 24, 25
  enzymes 17
  food-poisoning bacteria 20–1
  food spoilage 16–17, 18–19
  in foods 12–13
  growth 17, 18, 20, 21
  kitchen surfaces 22, 23
  Psychrobacter 17
  spores 23
  wastes 12, 17
beers and wines 11
biofilms 24–5
bread making 10, 11

Campylobacter 20, 28
canned foods 19
carbon dioxide 10, 11
cells 5, 10
  yeast cells 10, 11
cheese 9, 12, 13, 17
cheese mites 9
chopping boards 22, 23
cilia 25, 26, 27
ciliates 25, 28
Clostridium botulinum 21
clothes, sponges, and dish
  towels 4, 23
curds 13

disinfectants and bleaches 25
drains 2–5, 26, 27
dried foods 18
dust 6–7
dust mites 7, 28

eggs
  of dust mites 7
  of flour mites 8
  of rotifers 26
electron microscope 5
energy 10, 11
Enterobacter cloacae 23
enzymes 17
Escherichia coli 21

fermentation 11, 12, 13
flour mites 8
food poisoning 20–1
food preparation and storage
  17, 21
food spoilage 14–19
  bacteria 16–17, 18–19
  molds 14–15
  preventing 18–19
freeze-dried foods 18
frozen foods 18
fungi 5
  molds 13, 14–15, 23, 28
  parasites 15
  yeasts 10–11, 28

hand washing 23

garbage (kitchen) 22, 23

irradiation 19

kitchen cleaning 23
kitchen surfaces 22–3

lactic acid 13
Lactobacillus 12, 28

microbes 5
  in drains 24–5
  in foods 10-13
  on kitchen surfaces 22–3
  see also bacteria; fungi;
  protozoa
microscopes 5
  electron microscope 5
  light microscope 5

milk 12, 13, 16, 21
mites 7–9
  cheese mites 9
  droppings of 7, 9
  dust mites 7, 28
  eggs of 7, 8
  flour mites 8
molds 13, 14–15, 23, 28
  hyphae 14, 15
  spores 14, 15

oxygen 11

parasites 15
penicillin 14
Penicillium 14, 15, 28
pesticides 8
pickled foods 18
pollen 7
protozoans 25, 26
  amoebas 24, 25, 28
  ciliates 25, 28

refrigerators and freezers 17,
  18
rennet 13
rotifers 26–7, 28

Salmonella 21
salted foods 19
scrap buckets 22
skin flakes 6, 7
spores
  bacterial spores 23
  fungal spores 14, 15
Staphylococcus aureus 20
starch 11
Streptococcus thermophilis 12

toxins 20, 21

water vapor 7
whey 13

yeasts 10-11, 28
yogurt 12, 13, 17